Labrador Retriever

Charles and Linda George

Created by Q2AMedia
www.q2amedia.com
Editor Jeff O' Hare
Publishing Director Chester Fisher
Client Service Manager Santosh Vasudevan
Project Manager Kunal Mehrotra
Art Director Harleen Mehta
Designer Deepika Verma
Picture Researcher Nivisha Sinha

Library of Congress Cataloging-in-Publication Data
Labrador retriever / [Charles George, Linda George].
p. cm. — (Top dogs)
Includes index.
ISBN 0-531-23244-1/ 978-0-531-23244-6 (hardcover)
1. Labrador retriever—Juvenile literature. I. Title.
SF429.L3L327 2010
636.752'7—dc22
2010035034

This edition published by Scholastic Inc.,

Printed and bound in Heshan, China
232580 10/10
10 9 8 7 6 5 4 3 2 1

Picture Credits
t= top, b= bottom, c= center, r= right, l= left

Cover Page: Christopher Appoldt/Photolibrary

Title Page: Argo/Shutterstock

4-5: Mladen Mitrinovic/Shutterstock; 4l: Erik Lam/Shutterstock; 4r: Erik Lam/Shutterstock;
5l: Devin Koob/Shutterstock; 6: Ian Logan/Photographer's Choice/Getty Images; 7: Pressmaster/
Fotolia; 8-9: Val Lawless/Shutterstock; 8: Artem Kursin/Shutterstock; 9: Aleksandar Zoric/
Dreamstime; 10-11: Lunamarina/Dreamstime; 12-13: Yegorius/Shutterstock; 12: CarlssonInc/
Istockphoto; 13: Suto Norbert/123RF; 14-15: Mike Dabell/Istockphoto; 16-17: Argo/
Shutterstock; 17: Petspicture/Shutterstock; 18-19: Juniors Bildarchiv/Photolibrary;
19: Viorel Sima/Istockphoto; 20: Jon Labram/Istockphoto; 20-21: Cpaquin/Istockphoto;
22: Andersen Ross/Photolibrary; 23: Brand X Pictures/Photolibrary; 24-25: Nick Hayes/
Photolibrary; 26: Jan Paul Schrage/Photolibrary; 27: Kirk Geisler/Photolibary; 28: Lars
Christenen/123RF; 29: Karam Miri/Photolirbary; 30-31: Mike Hollist/Daily Mail/Rex Features.

Q2AMedia Art Bank: 5.

Contents

What Are Labrador Retrievers?

People in the U.S. love Labrador Retrievers. They are America's favorite **breed** of dog. More people in the U.S. have Labrador Retrievers than any other kind of dog. Most people call them Labs.

Fast Fact

Labs come in three colors. Some are black. Some are yellow. Others are dark brown, like chocolate.

Labs first came from Canada. They were **trained** to pick up animals and birds that hunters shot. The Labs also brought back fish. They loved to be in the water. They could even pull small fishing boats.

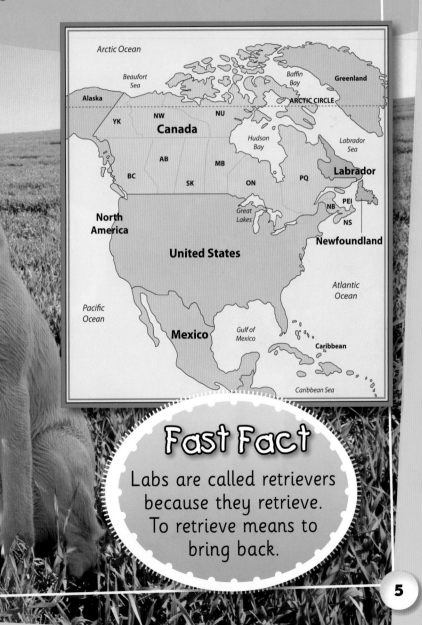

Arctic Ocean

Beaufort Sea

Baffin Bay

Greenland

Alaska

ARCTIC CIRCLE

YK

NW

NU

Canada

Hudson Bay

Labrador Sea

AB

MB

BC

SK

ON

PQ

Labrador

PEI

North America

Great Lakes

NB

NS

United States

Newfoundland

Atlantic Ocean

Pacific Ocean

Mexico

Gulf of Mexico

Caribbean

Caribbean Sea

Fast Fact

Labs are called retrievers because they retrieve. To retrieve means to bring back.

Puppy Love

Lab puppies are very cute. At birth, they weigh about 10-14 ounces (0.3-0.4 kg). Their eyes are closed when they are born. Their eyes won't open for at least fourteen days. Never open a puppy's eyes before they open on their own. You could make the puppy blind.

Fast Fact
Lab puppies have a sweet smell.

Puppies **nurse** or drink milk from their mothers for about six weeks. After that, they can eat special puppy food. Puppies play hard and then they sleep. They wake up, ready to play again.

Fast Fact
Eat, play, sleep. Puppies do this over and over. Eat! Play! Sleep!

Choosing a Lab Puppy

Fast Fact

There are usually seven or eight Lab puppies in a litter, but there can be more!

Puppies are born in a group called a **litter**. Watch how puppies in a litter play with each other. Which ones are playful? Which ones are quiet? If your family likes to run and play, choose a puppy with lots of energy.

A Lab puppy plays with its brothers and sisters a lot. Sometimes, their play can get a little rough. Some puppies push their playmates over! They also like to chew on each other's ears!

Fast Fact

Male Labs are more active than **female** Labs. A female Lab might be best for a quiet family.

Taking Care of Your Lab Puppy

When Lab puppies grow bigger, their teeth grow in. Then, they can eat puppy food from a bag or a can. They should eat food that's made just for puppies.

Fast Fact

Don't let your puppy chew anything that might hurt it.

Keep your Lab puppy warm and dry. It should have its own bed. When it is bigger, it can sleep at the foot of your bed. A Lab can live outside. But, it will be happier living inside with the people it loves.

Labs Love Kids!

A Lab will be good with children. But don't pull your Lab's ears or tail. This might hurt! Treat your puppy with kindness. If you do, your puppy will be nice to you, too.

Fast Fact

Puppies love to roll. They love having their tummies rubbed!

Labs won't bite, even when teased. Labs like playing with children. They like to run. They don't mind noise. Labs make good friends for kids.

Fast Fact

Play chase with your Lab! Roll on the ground with your dog. Have fun!

Full-Grown Labs

Labs are medium-sized dogs. Male Labs grow to be 22-25 inches (56-63.5 cm) tall. They weigh between 65 and 80 pounds (29-36 kg). Female Labs grow to be 21-24 inches (53-61 cm) tall. They weigh between 55 and 70 pounds (25-32 kg).

Labs look friendly. Their eyes show how smart they are. They watch everything that happens around them. Adult Labs have thick tails.

Fast Fact

A Lab's tail helps it to move about in water.

Brushing Hair and Clipping Nails

Labs have short, thick hair. Their hair stays smooth and flat. Labs should be gently brushed once a week. Brushing removes loose hair. Labs **shed** hair all the time.

Fast Fact

Labrador Retrievers shed a lot of hair in the spring. In the fall, their hair gets thicker.

A Lab's nails can tear or break when it runs. Running on rocks can shred the nails. They should be trimmed to keep them smooth. A veterinarian can do the trimming for you. A veterinarian is a doctor for animals.

Fast Fact

Your veterinarian will also give your Lab its shots. They keep your dog healthy.

Those Frisky Labs!

Fast Fact
Your Lab may need help climbing out of a swimming pool.

A Lab has lots of energy. It loves to run, play, and swim. Do you have a swimming pool, or a park with a lake nearby? If you do, your Lab could go swimming! Throw a ball into the water. Your Lab will jump in to get the ball.

Throw a ball, and your Lab will chase it. It will bring the ball back again and again. Keep throwing the ball! Your Lab also loves to go on walks and runs. A Lab needs a lot of **exercise**.

Fast Fact

A Lab that can't run and play may get bored. A dog that gets bored sometimes causes trouble.

Make Room for Your Lab!

A Lab can live in a small home. It will like running in a big fenced yard. If your yard isn't very big, your Lab will need to go for a walk every day.

Fast Fact

A **harness** may be better for your Lab than a collar. A collar can choke your dog if it pulls hard on the **leash**.

Some Labs live outside all the time. Labs that live outside should have a doghouse. Labs don't like hot weather. Be sure to give all dogs plenty of cool water to drink.

Fast Fact

During the hot summer, your Lab should have a cool place to take a nap.

Smart Dogs!

Labs are very smart. They are easy to train. Teach your Lab words like "No!" and "Come!" It will learn by hearing the words over and over.

Fast Fact

Never hit your dog. Instead, **scold** it if it does something wrong.

A Lab loves learning new things. Give your Lab a treat or a pat when it does something right. You can teach your dog to "Sit," "Stay," or "Roll over". Show your dog what you want it to do when you say the words.

Fast Fact

Your Lab will learn that "Supper!" means it's time to eat!

Hunting Dogs

Labs are great hunting dogs. They are not
afraid when they hear a gun. They like to
find and bring back birds or small animals.
They are not nervous dogs. They can be
comfortable in many different places.

Labs don't eat the animals they retrieve. They hold them gently in their mouths. Then, they drop the animal at the hunter's feet. Labs have strong jaws. They can carry large birds.

Fast Fact

A lot of hunters hunt big birds called geese. A Lab can carry one of these heavy birds.

Labs Helping People

Labs are working dogs. Labs like to work for their owners. They also can be **guide dogs**. Guide dogs help people who cannot see. Labs can also be trained to help people who are in wheelchairs. These dogs are called **service dogs**.

Fast Fact

Guide dogs lead their owners away from danger. They help them cross the street safely.

Labs can smell things that people cannot smell. Labs can be trained to sniff out drugs or bombs. Sometimes, they bark if they smell what they are looking for. At other times, they may sit down to signal to their owner that they have found something.

Fast Fact

Labs can also be **search and rescue dogs**. They search for people who are lost.

Best of the Breed

Endal was a service dog in England. He was very smart. Endal's owner was in a wheelchair. He taught Endal to understand more than 200 words. Once, Endal's owner had trouble putting a card into a bank slot. Endal took the card and put it in the slot. When money came out, Endal took it in his mouth and handed it to his owner.

Fast Fact

Endal's owner did not teach his dog how to put the card in the slot. Endal just knew!

No other dog has earned as many awards as Endal. He even has his own website! Endal's puppies are also service dogs.

Fast Fact

Another famous Lab is Marley. *Marley and Me* is a movie about a yellow Lab. Marley does crazy things in that movie!

Glossary

Breed – type of dog

Exercise – activities that works a dog's muscles

Female – a girl

Guide dog – a dog trained to help a person who cannot see

Harness – a set of straps that fit around a dog's chest and neck

Leash – a strap, attached to a collar or harness, used to help control a dog on a walk

Litter – a group of puppies born to one mother, at one time

Loyal – faithful

Male – a boy

Nurse – drink milk from a mother's breast

Scold – use an angry voice

Search and rescue dog – a dog trained to look for people who are lost

Service dog – a dog trained to help a person who cannot hear or who is in a wheelchair

Shed – lose hair

Trained – taught

Index